The thread is a thorn, but then it blooms

AF623598

Alexandra Weatherby

BookLeaf Publishing

The thread is a thorn, but then it blooms © 2023 Alexandra Weatherby

All rights reserved.

No part of this publication may be reproduced, stored in a retrieval system, or transmitted, in any form or by any means, electronic, mechanical, photocopying, recording or otherwise, without the prior written permission of the presenters.

Alexandra Weatherby asserts the moral right to be identified as author of this work.

Presentation by *BookLeaf Publishing*

Web: www.bookleafpub.com

E-mail: info@bookleafpub.com

ISBN: 9789357441315

First edition 2023

PREFACE

'The thread is a thorn, but then it blooms' captures the highs and lows of living with mental health struggles, and focuses on self-growth by learning to be present, practicing gratitude, self compassion, and proactively stepping out of your comfort zone.

The thread is a thorn

Hanging on
by a thread,
but the thread
is a thorn

The longer
you hold on
the bigger
the wound becomes,
and the more painful
it gets

But the wound
is where the light enters
and where there is light
there is growth

And where there is growth
things begin to bloom

Because the thread
is a thorn,
but then
it blooms

Anchor

A fast falling
downward spiral

A heaviness
so strong
and so tight
pulling me down
into the deepest
and darkest
parts
of myself

Retreating
inside myself
and burrowing
so much so
that you begin
to forget
who
you once were
like a polaroid
fading
through time

Safe,
but lonely
and continually
sinking,
constantly
waiting
for the heaviness
to lighten,
for the storm
to subside

For someone
or something
to weigh anchor
and set me free

To hoist me up
or wash me ashore,
to carry me home
back
to myself
whole
at last

De pression

'Pression',
is an act
of applying
pressure

So 'de pression'
is an act
of not
applying pressure

Depression
feeds off
inaction;
a lack of doing
a lack of moving
a lack of hope
a lack of joy

To begin
an upward spiral,
to build up
momentum,
you must start
by applying
positive
pressure

To combat
depression
is to implement
self compassion

To love yourself
like a friend
because you only have
one home,
and to lose yourself
is to be homeless,
an empty vessel
a mind
and body
separate
and divided
forever

Anxius

Anxiety
anxious
'anxius'
'anxietas'
'ankho',
to choke
to distress
to worry
to dwell

Anxiety
it thrives
off your breath,
or lack of
should I say

To breathe
in moments
of turmoil
is the greatest
resistance
of all

To breathe
in moments
of anxiety
is to starve
anxiety
of oxygen,
'to choke'
anxiety
back

Oxygen tank

Living
with anxiety
as well as
depression
is like
swimming
in the ocean
with
an oxygen tank

A heaviness
that follows
you around
wherever
you go

A constant fear
and lack of hope
that's slowly
robbing you
of your oxygen

But the slower
you breathe
and the calmer
you remain
the more oxygen
you get to keep
and the more you can travel
the depths of the ocean
while still having
enough oxygen
to return back
safely
to the boat
ready
to go again

OCD

Like a mosquito bite,
an itch you cannot scratch
a thirst you cannot quench
an addiction you cannot stop

An insatiable yearning
for a sense of relief

An attempt to self soothe
to try to feel at peace
or in control,
that soon spirals
into an obsession
a compulsion
a nervous tic
a habit
a routine
that you cannot break

A heightened sense of blame
an overestimation of threat
inflated responsibility
intrusive thoughts
nonsensical worrying
driven by fear

A consistent feeling
of treading on eggshells

A seed of doubt
growing uncontrollably
like a swarm of bees
you can't shake off
stinging, burning
burrowing
into every crevice of your mind
festering
continuously

Danger
dread
anxiety
a whirlwind of emotions
all at once
forcing you
to overthink
over plan
over prepare,
a constant niggling of
'what if?'
on repeat
like a merry-go-round
whirling
forever in your mind

Panic attack

A ball of yarn
in the palm of your hand
that's there one second
and gone the next,
snatched
from your grip
like a bolting horse
and its reigns

Blindsided,
a complete loss of control
a knot in your chest
so painful
that you can barely breathe
even just
a shallow breath,
a knot
so tight
and tangled
and constantly growing
getting larger
and larger
every time
with every breath,
slowly suffocating

and choking you

Like an electric shock,
or a needle and thread
being pulled
slowly
through your heart
and dissipating
through your shoulder
fizzling out
and spreading
to every single cell
in your body
as if there's a poison
travelling
through your veins
like a snake
injecting its venom
whilst simultaneously
wrapping itself
around your lungs,
all within
the blink
of an eye

Flooded and burnt

Flooded
and burnt
broken
and wounded

An influx
of emotion
washing
all over you,
a sobering sensation
an enlivening experience
to feel
so deeply
and simultaneously,
an almost
pleasant moment
bewildered
and beguiled,
deceived
by the fascination
to feel
so intensely
amazed
by your own mind

and its ability
to amalgamate
such a strong fusion
of emotions,
so much so
that you forget
how overwhelming it is
to feel flooded
by despair
dread
and anxiety,
and burnt
by anguish
outrage
and envy

The climb

A mountain
rocky and steep
slippery
from the torrential downpour
of rain,
trying to hold on
but you lose your grip
falling fast
and landing
back
to where you started

Badly bruised
but not broken
and unwilling
to give up,
you carry on
with the climb
stepping into
the unknown
like a blindfolded
soldier
in the middle
of a war

The sky above you
is a canvas of white
speckled
with grey stains
that smudge
and blur
into a vast
colour-less palette
lifeless
and apathetic

A whistle of wind
and the storm starts again
like a dormant volcano
patiently waiting
to erupt
with its smothering ash-cloud
and destructive lava
overflowing
and seeping
through every crack
and crevice,
punishing you
for the ignored signals
and the silenced alarms
that lit the fuse
and allowed it
to explode

Like a tornado
chewing up
and spitting out
anything
in its path
forcing you
to pick up the pieces
and to confront
the parts of you
that are gone

Hidden
from your line of vision
yet still there
in plain sight,
the parts of you
were never gone
they were just buried
within the debris
misplaced
and wounded
and waiting
to be found

Weathering the storm within

Paradise
is sunshine,
palm trees
whistling
in the wind,
a gentle breeze
cascading over you,
sand
between your toes,
a glistening sea
twinkling
in the reflection
of the sun,
a blinding glow
so warm
and bright
that everything
it touches
is tinted
with gold

A small gust
of wind,
a thickening blanket
of cloud

that's darkening
into a shade of grey
that's so dark
it's like charcoal

A drizzle of rain
that quickly turns
into a monsoon,
a constant downpour
that seems
so never ending
that you begin
to find comfort
in its stability,
a sense of calm
knowing
and trusting
that the storm
will always be there,
unrelenting
and determined
to sound every alarm
that's inside of you
until every part
of your body
knows
of its presence,
a caution
a warning

to go
no further
until
the storm
has passed

The lobster

The lobster,

sharp
and snappy
with daggers
for claws

Feared
by others,
forever pushing you
away

Defensive
and indenial,
avoidant
and insecure,
petrified of failure
protecting itself
with its claws,
blaming
stonewalling
gaslighting
them all,
the lobster
that fears

pain
most of all

Scared
of vulnerability
it shuts them out
once more,
thinking
that all the pain
would avoid it
for sure

But the pain
snook in,
stealthily
undetected,
and the lobster
was lonely,
and unloved
once more

But the thing
with lobsters
is that pain
follows them everywhere,
there's a comfort
in the inevitability,
a liberation
in the epiphany

So the lobster
changes,
transforming
for good,
shedding
its shell,
and growing
once more

The wilted rose

Red with fire,
pink with love,
a rose
of wonder,
a rainbow
of passion

The rose
that blossoms
year
after year
from summer
through winter
a resilience
so pure

There's a peace
in knowing
it will come back
once more,
for nothing
in nature
truly blooms
all year,
for even the rose

is wilted
in spite
of standing tall,
like a beacon of hope
a journey
a cycle
that's transcendent
of life,
like a soul that leaves us
yet lives forever,
watching over you
while you're sleeping,
among us
forever,
a love
that is never lost
only waiting
to be found,
for the rose
is that symbol
of a love
that's forever bound

No rain, no flowers

Have you ever wondered
why
you love the sound of rain

its because
the chaos
is outside of you
its running down your window
its drizzling over your hair

its because
without the rain
there would be
no flowers

without the rain,
there would only be
sunshine,
and nothing
would ever grow

without the rain,
the storm,
and the numbing
grey skies,

no-one
would ever smile
when the sunshine
finally came

Cherophobia

A fear
of happiness
so deep
that
it touches
every fibre
of your being

It closes off
parts of your soul
like a gardener
dead-heading
every
one
of their plants

It stains
your memory

It darkens
every blue sky

It robs you
of joy
like a thief

in the night.

A fear
so strong
that you surrender
every time

A fear
of loving
that stems from
a fear
of losing

A fear
of choosing
and never
being chosen

A fear of
abandonment,
rejection,
detachment

A fear
that holds
every key
to your heart,
terrified
of being opened,

too scared
to dare
to love.

A fear
that slowly
starts to shrink

A fear
that eventually
diminishes

A fear
that finally
cracks
and breaks
into a thousand
tiny pieces

Pieces
that blossom
and grow
into love

A love
that is freeing
enlivening
uplifting
empowering

A love
that is
so pure
its intoxicating
like a hunger
you can never
fulfil

A love
so strong
that it is
worth
the risk of
losing
it all.

Significant other

Significant other
significant lover
illimitably yours
forever

With eyes so bright
and a whispering sprinkle of blue,
like ice
so debilitating
and mesmerising
all at once

With lips
so soft
and so gentle
they give you goosebumps
every time,
butterflies in your stomach,
and a shiver
down your spine

With hands
that touch you
and arms
that hold you

that whisk you
off your feet
until you feel
as light
as a feather

Opening your heart
like the key
to a door
familiar
and fitting
together
as one,
like two pieces
of the same puzzle
irregular
different
yet the same,
standing alone
they shine
strong
and independent,
but together
they are unified
whole
and complete,
a perfect mix
a balance
of opposites

complimenting
and counteracting
each other,
sharing their strengths
and halving
their weaknesses,
a love
so pure
that it will
endure

Dragonfly

Humming
and buzzing
hovering
from above
the stream
that guides you
whistling
to go on

Like a bird
in solitude
singing
its own duet,
the dragonfly
no longer
seeks
that you accept.

A new love
that is found
nearby a river
without a sound,
with all
but a whisper,

a softening
sweet sound

A sense of calm
tranquility
and peace,
the dragonfly
wonders
when
this will cease

A home
by the water
can never subside
the storm that will find you,
rising
the tide

For the rain
that will pour
forever
and once more,
the dragonfly
must prosper
forgetting
about the storm

For the storm
shall pass

when an anchor
is cast,
when it's safe
to explore
the dragonfly
goes ashore

Forever
exploring
and transforming
once more,
the dragonfly
changes
constantly searching
for more

Kingfisher

A rainbow of feathers,
a multi-coloured missile
diving into the water
blindfolded,
they prowl

Tiny
yet mighty,
fragile
yet firm,
a bird
so speedy
all you see
is a whirl

A whirl full of orange
turquoise
and teal blue,
the kingfisher
is a symbol
of free spirit
that's anew

An emblem
of abundance,

prosperity
and love,
with freedom
and courage,
wanderlust
running in their blood

They bring
good fortune,
they're a story
to follow,
they're an example
to live by,
because they take away
your sorrow

For the kingfisher's
prowess
at dancing
in the rain
is a reminder
of adventure,
and to never
live in vain

Bloom

A flower
starts off
as a seed
with roots
that grow
with a hunger
for a life
full of wonder

A flower
that blossoms
with stems
so strong
with a thirst
for adventure
and a desire
to prosper

With a longing
to feel
so deeply
and intensely,
you were warned
to be careful,
a caution

what to wish for

For when the sun
starts to fade,
and when the clouds
begin to thicken,
you will long
for protection
from the storm
that's yet to form

A naive flower
so innocent
and pure
with a gift
for giving
that never questioned
who wanted more,
with a love
for loving,
you were forever
blindsided,
forever kept
in the dark,
like a fire
without a spark

But then
the rain came

with the moon
and the stars,
guiding you back
to your roots,
protecting you
from afar,
watering your soil,
feeding your roots,
the sun shines above you
whispering
encouraging
for you to bloom

www.ingramcontent.com/pod-product-compliance
Lightning Source LLC
Chambersburg PA
CBHW051743130826
49812CB00033B/978
* 9 7 8 9 3 5 7 4 4 1 3 1 5 *